God
is
Always There

Jennifer McCaskill

Liberation's Publishing LLC ~ West Point, MS
ISBN: 13: 978-0692537893
EBook ISBN: 978-0-9891348-1-1

Dedication

I would like to Thank and dedicate this book to my Precious and Sweet Almighty GOD for HIS unfailing, never-ending, and strong love, who is Lord and Savior over my life. HALLELUJAH!!!!! I want to thank and dedicate my book to my parents James and Joan Beamon for teaching me about the love of Christ and being such an excellent role model for me. For giving me such a wonderful life as a child and being there for me as an adult. To my children Joshua I. Kitchens and Abigail E. McCaskill for being such a blessing to me.

The Lord knows what we need and I thank HIM for blessing me with such sweet and beautiful children. My siblings James Eric Beamon and Joyce Annette Beamon-Alston, I love you guys. To my nephews Timothy, Caleb and my niece Jasmine, Tee-tee love you all deeply. I want to say to my Grandmothers Willie M. Beason and Esther L. Rankin I love you forever and always. I can't end before sending a thank you to heaven to my Aunt Martha M. Williams and my first cousin Sundra M. Williams (little sister) for having such a profound impact on my life. I want to Thank my church family Mount Pleasant M.B. Church of Chesterville Belden, MS for their kindness and love. I truly thank God for my pastor and wife Henry L. and Linda Vaughn for being a true man and woman of God and showing us the meaning of love.

I must remember my youth minister and wife Rev. Stephen and Tandalya Traylor for being such a good role model to my daughter and the other youth in our church and community. Thanks to my home church Marble Rock M.B. Church for my foundation. Lastly, my supporters for believing in me and allowing GOD to show to you that I am a willing vessel who deeply loves the Lord and is ready to be used by HIM! I dedicate this book to all of you.

Miracles and Blessings!

WORDS OF ENCOURAGMENT

I encourage you on a daily basis to pray and ask God to give you the strength to do His will. Also, remember to help others and be a blessing to them. We are living in a time where people are hurting and they need you and truthfully, You need them. We are not here just for ourselves. We can't help others on our strength but only through God. We must also remember that only what we do for Christ will last. Keep praying, trusting, and believing. GOD knows what you need and HE is working on your behalf. HE loves you and so do I.

love forever,
Jennifer

PRAYER

Heavenly Father, I come to You as humble as I know how expressing to You my heartfelt thanks, to You and Your Son Jesus for your countless wonderful Blessings. LORD, You are Awesome and there are no words to truly describe Your Awesomeness. LORD GOD, I ask You to continue blessing Your children with good health, strength, sound mind and a loving heart. I ask you Dear Master to allow Your Words, to touch the hearts of men/women. I pray, that the words that I received from you through this book, will deliver Your people, from any situation that is causing them not to trust You and is holding them back from serving You.

I ask this in Your Son Jesus name.

Amen

When your health is
failing...

God

is there.

When there's trouble at school...

God

is there.

When there's trouble on
your job...

God

is there.

When you're hurting and
no one seems to care...

God

is there.

When you're feeling
hopeless...

God

is there.

When your parents just
don't understand what
you're feeling...

God

is there.

When your heart is
broken, and there is a
feeling of void in your life...

God

is there.

When you are restless...

God

is there.

When you are feeling
worthless...

God

is there.

When your friends turn
their backs on you...

God

is there.

When you are spiritually
broken...

God

is there.

When your loved ones are
called home to be with the
LORD...

God

is there.

When you can't find your
way along life's journey...

God

is there.

When you can't find
peace in your life...

God

is there.

When you don't know
which way to turn...

God

is there.

When you're fighting depression...

God

is there.

When you are fearful...

God

is there.

When you're going
through a divorce...

God

is there.

When you're going
through a custody battle...

God

is there.

When you're battling
sexual demons...

God

is there.

When you are weary...

God

is there.

When you are confused...

God

is there.

When you have to care for
your loved ones...

God

is there.

When you are weak and
worn...

God

is there.

When you are torn...

God

is there.

When you're fighting
addictions...

God

is there.

When you are a single
parent...

God

is there.

When there is trouble in
your marriage or
relationship...

God

is there.

Through all of life's trial
and Tribulations...
You
Must
Tell
Yourself

God is there!

God is there!

God

is there!!!

It's important to remember that whatever you are going through God is there and is able to see you through. You must trust God first, for Who HE is and trust that HE will Never Leave nor Forsake You. Jesus knows your fears and griefs. You are to cast your cares upon HIM, for HE cares for you and if it isn't true HE, wouldn't have told you.

"And Jesus came and spoke unto them, saying, All power is given unto me in heaven and in earth." Matthew 28:18 This tells you that God has ALL Power and only HE can turn any and every situations around.

Always remember to Trust God for Everything and Surrender to HIS will for your life. Only then will you experience the true meaning of Peace and HE will pour out HIS abundance of Blessings according to HIS will for your life.

"Teaching them to observe all things whatsoever I have commanded you: and, lo, I am with you Always, even unto the end of the world." Matthew 28:20 This tells You that you, are never alone and that God is Always there. SHOUT HALLELUJAH!!!!!!! This was true then and is still true Today. God can't and will not Change.

THIS IS YOUR PRAISE BREAK. You should start to feel the chains falling NOW in just knowing that GOD is always there. Give GOD your best praise!! SHOUT HALLELUJAH, SHOUT VICTORY, CLAIM YOUR HEALING IN THE NAME OF JESUS. DO YOUR PRAISE DANCE, RELEASE THE BURDENS THAT HAD YOU BOUND. STRAIGHTING UP AND LIFT YOUR HEAD. HALLELUJAH!

I pray that you received confirmation and a healing from the words of this book. I also, pray the blessings of the Lord upon You and your life. May God enrich your life with his wonderful, blessed and powerful words and Blessings. Miracles are preformed every day and you are next. It is important that you have the faith to believe that. Remember GOD is not just there,

HE'S ALWAYS THERE!

Jennifer Ann Beamon-McCaskill

Born in Kosciusko, MS on December 13, 1974 now resides in Tupelo, MS. She is a Phlebotomist and has been in the health care field for 19 years. She is also a Mary Kay Beauty Consultant and enjoy meeting and working with different women to help build self-esteem and self-confidence. Jennifer has two children a son Joshua, who attends a University in the state of MS and a daughter Abigail, who is in high school. She sings in the church choir and is a part of the praise team. She is a member of the Women of Grace ministry in her church and acts as church secretary.

Jennifer loves the Lord and loves to help people. " I often tell people about helping others on a daily basis, We are not here unto ourselves but to help other, That's required of us." " I plan as long as it's GOD plan for my life to help others and to lead individuals to Christ and the best example should, start with me."

Jennifer is now starting on a new book and plans to start a project that will center around the less fortunate and elderly.

contact information:
mccaskilljennifer@yahoo.com
Phone 662-341-5991